PROMINENT WOMEN IN HISTORY (continued)

Victoria	1819–1901	Long-reigning English queen; inspired "Victorian era"
Florence Nightingale	1820–1910	Italian-British nurse; founded nursing as a profession
Susan B. Anthony	1820–1906	American suffragette, women's rights advocate
Elizabeth Blackwell	1821–1910	First woman doctor in the United States
Harriet Tubman	c.1820–1913	Antislavery activist, "conductor" of Underground Railroad
Antoinette Blackwell	1825–1921	First American woman to become ordained minister
Josephine Butler	1828–1906	Victorian society critic, advocate for prostitutes
Mary "Mother" Jones	1830–1930	American labor organizer, agitator for union rights
Belva Lockwood	1830–1917	First woman lawyer to argue a U.S. Supreme Court case
Queen Liliuokalani	1838–1917	Last Hawaiian monarch to govern the islands
Victoria Woodhull	1838–1927	American social reformer, women's rights advocate
Ellen Richards	1842–1911	American chemist, founder of home economics
Sarah Winnemucca	c. 1844–1891	Native American educator, tribal leader
Carry Nation	1846–1911	American writer, temperance advocate
Kate Chopin	1851–1904	American feminist author; wrote *The Awakening* (1899)
Queen Min	1851–1895	Korean queen; forged stronger ties with Russia
Emmeline Pankhurst	1858–1928	English suffragette, Independent Labor Party member
Pandita Ramabai	1858–1922	Indian Sanskrit scholar; feminist critic of Hinduism
Jane Addams	1860–1935	American social reformer; cofounded Hull House
Kishida Toshiko	1863–1901	Japanese leader of women's rights campaigns
Marie Curie	1867–1934	Polish-French physical chemist; discovered radioactivity
Nellie Bly	1867–1922	American newspaper writer; circled globe in record time
Raden Ajeng Kartini	1879–1904	Outspoken Indonesian activist; started girls' school
Margaret Sanger	1879–1966	American pioneer of birth control movement
Eleanor Roosevelt	1884–1962	American first lady, diplomat, social reformer
Alice Paul	1885–1977	American suffragette, social reformer
Amelia Earhart	1897–1937	American aviator; first woman to fly solo across Atlantic
Golda Meir	1898–1978	Russian-born prime minister of Israel
Margaret Mead	1901–1978	American anthropologist, author; questioned femininity
Maggie Kuhn	1905–1995	American social activist, advocate for elderly rights
Simone de Beauvoir	1908–1986	French radical intellectual; wrote *The Second Sex* (1949)
Lucille Ball	1911–1989	American comic actress and television star
Babe Didrikson Zaharias	1914–1956	American multisport athlete; won several gold medals
Indira Gandhi	1917–1984	Prime minister of India; social reformer
Eva Perón	1919–1952	Actress, controversial first lady of Argentina
Betty Friedan	1921–	American activist; wrote *The Feminine Mystique*; founded NOW
Helen Gurley Brown	1922–	American writer, editor; founded *Cosmopolitan* magazine
Margaret Thatcher	1925–	English politician; first woman prime minister in Europe
Althea Gibson	1927–2003	American tennis player; first black woman to win 3 titles
Maya Angelou	1928–	American poet, memoirist; spoke at Clinton's inauguration
Mary Daly	1928–	American radical feminist, cultural critic, writer
Dolores Huerta	1930–	American labor leader, activist for migrant farm workers
Luce Irigaray	1930–	French feminist philosopher, critic, writer
Corazón Aquino	1933–	President of Philippines; oversaw new constitution
Audre Lorde	1934–1992	American black lesbian poet, novelist, essayist
Kate Millet	1934–	American author; wrote *Sexual Politics* (1970)
Gloria Steinem	1934–	American political activist, editor; founded *Ms.* magazine
Monique Wittig	1935–2003	French avant-garde novelist, writer, critic, scholar
Valerie Solanas	1936–1988	American radical; wrote *SCUM Manifesto*; shot Andy Warhol
Hélène Cixous	1937–	French critic, playwright, novelist, scholar
Valentina Tereshkova	1937–	Russian cosmonaut; first woman to travel in space
Judy Chicago	1939–	American artist; founded Feminist Studio Workshop
Germaine Greer	1939–	Australian sexual freedom activist; wrote *The Female Eunuch*
Wilma Rudolph	1940–1994	American athlete; won three track-and-field gold medals
Julia Kristeva	1941–	French critic, psychoanalyst, semiotician, writer
Robin Morgan	1941–	American civil rights advocate, lesbian feminist
Gloria Anzaldúa	1942–2004	Mexican-American writer, scholar, cultural theorist, critic
Gayatri Spivak	1942–	Indian-American literary theorist, cultural critic, scholar
Janis Joplin	1943–1970	American rock and blues singer, activist; died of overdose
Billie Jean King	1943–	American tennis player; elevated women's status in sport
Angela Davis	1944–	American militant black activist; tried for conspiracy
Donna Haraway	1944–	American feminist theorist; wrote *Cyborg Manifesto*
Aung San Suu Kyi	1945–	Burmese peace advocate; won Nobel Peace Prize in 1991
Wilma Mankiller	1945–	Native American activist; first woman chief of Cherokee
Catherine MacKinnon	1946–	American radical feminist, pornography critic, lawyer
Andrea Dworkin	1946–	American radical feminist, pornography critic, writer
Seyla Benhabib	1950–	Turkish-American feminist theorist, scholar, critic
Sally Ride	1951–	American; first U.S. woman in outer space
Patricia Williams	1951–	American; legal scholar; cultural critic; writer
bell hooks	1952–	American; black feminist scholar; feminist activist
Benazir Bhutto	1953–	Pakistani prime minister; first woman to lead a Muslim nation
Trinh T. Minh-Ha	1953–	Vietnamese-American filmmaker, social theorist, writer
Gayle Rubin	c. 1955–	American lesbian critic, scholar, writer
Judith Butler	1956–	American literary critic; theorized gender as performance

TYPES OF FEMINISM

Amazon feminism: Focuses on the image of the female hero, both fictional and real, in literature and art, and is particularly concerned with physical equality. Opposes gender role stereotypes and discrimination against women, particularly images of women as passive, weak, and physically helpless.

Anarcho-feminism: Anarchist branch of radical feminism based on the work of Emma Goldman. Focuses on critiquing society based on race, gender, and social class.

Cultural feminism: Focuses on women's inherent differences from men, including their "natural" kindness, tendencies to nurture, pacifism, relationship focus, and concern for others. Opposes an emphasis on equality and instead argues for increased value placed on culturally-designated "women's work."

Difference feminism: *See cultural feminism.* Emphasizes women's difference/uniqueness and traditionally "feminine" characteristics; argues that more value should be placed on these qualities.

Erotic feminism: German-based feminism emphasizing the philosophical, metaphysical, and life-creating value of erotic life. Argues that sexuality opposes war and is thus distinctly feminine.

Ecofeminism: Argues against patriarchal tendencies to destroy the environment, animals, and natural resources. Focuses on efforts to stop plundering of Earth's resources, often drawing parallels between exploitation of women and exploitation of the Earth. Frequently connected with spirituality and vegetarianism.

Equality feminism: Focuses on gaining equality between men and women in all domains (work, home, sexuality, law). Argues that women should receive all privileges given to men and that biological differences between men and women do not justify inequality. Most common form of feminism represented in the media.

Essentialist feminism: Focuses on "true" "biological" differences between men and women, arguing that women are essentially different from men but equal in value (i.e.,"separate but equal").

Feminazism: Militant form of radical feminism that embraces the hostile term "feminazi" (taken from the "Nazi" reference to fascism), originally and most often used as a hateful label for feminists. These feminists are often highly disliked by popular culture and ghettoized as "crazy," "outrageous," and "bitchy."

Feminism and women of color: Focuses on multiple forms of oppression (race and gender in particular, but also sexuality and social class). First feminism to draw attention to the whiteness of mainstream feminism and the need to look at race and gender.

Fourth-world feminism: Focuses on the power relationships between colonizers and (native) colonized people. Argues against the process of colonization, which native cultures are stripped of their customs, values, land, and traditions and forced to adopt the colonizers' ways of life.

French feminism: Movement by a set of French feminist thinkers (Julia Kristeva, Luce Irigaray, Simone de Beauvoir, Monique Wittig, Hélène Cixous, and others), mainly in the 1970s, who reshaped feminist thought by adding a philosophical focus to feminist theory. These feminists were associated with several male intellectuals of the time, including Derrida, Bataille, and Barthes.

Individual/libertarian feminism: Argues for minimal government intervention, anarchy, and an end to capitalism. Focuses on individual autonomy, rights, liberty, independence, and diversity.

Lesbian feminism: Diverse feminism based on the rejection of institutionalized heterosexism, particularly the primacy of the nuclear family, and the lack of legal recognition afforded to lesbians. Argues that lesbian identity is both personal and political, and actively works against homophobia.

Liberal feminism: *See equality feminism.* Focuses on working *within* institutions to gain equality for women (e.g., the vote, equal protection under the law) but does not focus on changing the entire institution (e.g., doing away with government). Often at odds with radical feminism.

Marxist/socialist feminism: Attributes women's oppression to a capitalist economy and the private property system. Argues that capitalism must be overthrown if the oppression of women is to end. Draws parallels between women and "workers" and emphasizes collective change rather than individual change.

Material feminism: Late 19th-century movement to liberate women by improving their material conditions, removing domestic responsibilities such as cooking and housework, and allowing women to earn their own wages.

Moderate feminism: Similar to liberal feminism; sees the importance of change within institutions. Argues for small steps toward gender equality. Often comprised of younger women who espouse feminist ideas without calling themselves "feminists."

Pop feminism: Focuses on caricatures of "girl power" idols and "Wonder Woman" images. Sometimes derided by feminists, but often attracts young women interested in empowerment but uninterested in social change and activism. Examples include *Powerpuff Girls, She-Ra, Buffy the Vampire Slayer,* and *Charlie's Angels.*

Postcolonial feminism: Emphasizes a rejection of colonial power relationships (in which the colonizer strips the colonized subject of her customs, traditions, and values). Argues for the deconstruction of power relationships and the inclusion of race within feminist analyses. Usually includes all feminist writings not from Britain or the United States.

Postfeminism: Feminism informed by psychoanalysis, postmodernism, and postcolonialism. Emphasizes multiple forms of oppression, multiple definitions of feminism, and a shift beyond equality as the major goal of the feminist movement.

Postmodern feminism: Critiques the male/female binary, and argues against this binary as the organizing force of society. Advocates deconstructionist techniques of blurring boundaries, eliminating dichotomies, and accepting multiple realities rather than searching for a singular "truth."

Psychoanalytic feminism: Uses psychoanalysis as a tool of female liberation by revising certain patriarchal tenants, such as Freud's view on mothering, Oedipal/Electra complex, penis envy, and female sexuality.

Radical feminism: Cutting-edge branch of feminism focused on sweeping social reforms, social change, and revolution. Argues against institutions like patriarchy, heterosexism, and racism and instead emphasizes gender as a social construction, denouncing biological roots of gender difference. Often paves the way for other branches of feminism.

Separatist feminism: Advocates separation from men, physically, emotionally, psychologically, and spiritually. Argues for women-only spaces, large and small, including lesbian separatist living communities, women-only music festivals, and consciousness-raising groups. Often emphasizes healing and connection between women that male-patriarchal spaces prohibit. Sometimes promotes spelling "women" as "womyn" in order to remove "men" from the word "women."

Socialist feminism: Blend of Marxist feminism and radical feminism. Argues against capitalism and for socialism, saying that collective efforts to overthrow existing economic systems ultimately will benefit women.

Third-world feminism: *See postcolonial feminism.* Emphasizes feminist scholarship outside Britain and the United States and the ways in which capitalism shapes all relationships of dominance. Shows how oppression of women by men is similar to oppression of third-world countries by first-world countries.

WOMEN'S STUDIES TERMINOLOGY

Anarchic: Informed by the belief that all government is undesirable.

Biopolitics: A theory that all forms of life are in some way political and therefore subject to debate, control, and regulation.

Canon/canonization: An official or authoritative list of important works in a given field; the process of making such list.

Cyborg: A symbolic representation of the merge between the human organism and some form of technology.

Deconstruction: A school of philosophy started in France during the 1960s; goal is to "undo" the Truth of a given text, to explode a single text into multiple texts in order to reveal its potential.

Dichotomy: A division of something into two mutually exclusive parts.

Discrimination: The continued treatment of a group on a basis other than individual merit.

Empower: To give authority or power to; to take power for one's own.

Epistemology: The study of how we know or gain knowledge. Feminist epistemology refers to the way feminists as a whole have constructed alternative forms of knowledge and self-expression.

Essentialism: A belief in the real, true essence of things; an investment in the invariable and fixed properties that define something.

Exoticization: The process by which a person or group of people is simultaneously sexualized and made "Other" (e.g., tourist brochures often exoticize Hawaiian women).

Feminization: The process by which something takes on the characteristics of the stereotypically feminine.

Fluid: Resisting one fixed and unchangeable form (e.g., fluid sexuality, fluid identity).

"The Gaze": The symbolic and literal act of looking at, and objectifying, those in a lower position of power than oneself.

Gender identity: The subjective but continuous, persistent sense of oneself as male or female.

Gender presentation: The presentation of one's gender through personality or bodily dress.

Gender roles: Behaviors, attitudes, values, or beliefs that a cultural group considers appropriate for males vs. females on the basis of biological sex (e.g., dolls vs. trucks, pink vs. blue).

Herstory vs. history: The conscious effort of feminist historians to revise the largely male narrative of *his*tory to include adequate representation of women and their legacy (*her*story).

Hierarchical binaries: The relationship between two opposite entities such that one becomes dominant and highly valued while the other becomes nondominant and devalued.

Identity politics: The examination of marginalized (nondominant) identities with the goal of challenging dominant categorizations while also asserting greater self-determination.

Logocentrism: A system of analysis focused on words and language at the exclusion of historical context or an author's individuality.

"The Man" (singular, capitalized): A symbolic reference to all institutionalized oppression (e.g., "working for The Man").

Marginalize: To relegate or confine to a lower or outer limit, edge, or inferior position.

Master narrative/metanarrative: The idea of one singular text that describes the course of history. This narrative tends to exclude the histories of oppressed peoples, including women, people of color, gays and lesbians, and the poor.

Matrilineal/matrilocal: Refers to kinship and descent traced through the mother.

Matrix theory of power: A theory of power diffuse in both its origins and operations, rather than a top-down process.

Naturalization vs. denaturalization: The process by which something takes on the characteristics of the innate, natural, or given (e.g., to naturalize sex roles) vs. the process by which the supposedly "natural" is constructed as social, changeable, and political (e.g., to denaturalize gender).

Nature/culture: A central and defining hierarchical binary that divides the world according to the natural, uncivilized, and barbaric versus the cultural, civilized, and refined.

Oppression: Cruel or unjust exercise of power or authority over others.

Other/Otherness/Othered (capitalized): Refers to the concept of difference or oppositeness from oneself, often with negative connotations. Can be used as a verb (to Other), noun (Other), or descriptive phrase (Otherness).

Patriarchal: Recognizing fathers, and all men, as the leaders and rulers of the family and society.

Patrilineal/patrilocal: Refers to kinship and descent traced through the father.

Penis envy: In psychoanalysis, the process by which young girls recognize their genitals as lacking a penis, and therefore develop envy of the size and symbolic power of the penis.

Performative: Having characteristics of a performance or show, despite being labeled as inherent, innate, or true by dominant culture (e.g., gender as performative).

Phallocentrism: Derived from the word "phallus" (male penis). This refers to something which is centered on men or a male viewpoint, especially related to the domination of women.

Phallogocentrism: A combination of phallocentrism and logocentrism, resulting in an ahistorical and noncontextualized view of male dominance, thus limiting and restricting knowledge while also forming the roots of women's oppression.

Postcolonialism: That which comes after, or reacts to, colonial rule; an intellectual movement drawing upon the scholarship of non-American and non-British scholars which is often highly critical of power, domination, oppression, and tyranny.

Postmodernism: Art and writing that rejects the modernist/classical principles of Truth and singular reality. Postmodernism instead argues for multiple forms of reality, blurred boundaries, no single Truth, and the necessity of subjective experience.

Psychoanalysis: A treatment for psychological disorders that focuses on early childhood, the unconscious, dreams, and subtexts of meaning.

Repression: Forcible subjugation or oppression; in psychoanalysis, the unconscious exclusion of painful feelings, impulses, and desires from the conscious mind.

Sex vs. gender: Sex refers to the biological aspects of being male or female; gender refers to the social aspects of being male or female.

Sexual identity: The "objective" characterization of one's physiological status as male or female.

Sexual orientation: Inclination toward same-sex and/or opposite-sex partners (e.g., homosexual, bisexual, heterosexual).

Sex role stereotype: The socially determined model that contains beliefs about what certain gender roles should be.

Sex typing: Differential treatment of people based on their biological sex.

Sexuality: The dimension of human existence involving sexual acts, preferences, behaviors, and identities.

Social constructionism: The dynamic process by which social phenomena (e.g., sexuality, money, marriage) are created, institutionalized, and made into tradition. Such phenomena often appear natural, inherent, or immutable, but in reality, are politically constituted, socially created, and potentially changeable.

Standpoint theory: A theory that oppressed people have access to particular kinds of unique knowledge not available to dominant groups.

Stereotyping: Consistent portrayal of traits about a group, which may be entirely or partly untrue.

Subaltern: Subordinate; outside of the established structure of political discourse and representation.

Subject/object: A central dichotomy in feminist theory, which posits that dominant groups (male, white, heterosexual) construct the reality of nondominant groups. Those in control of reality (subjects) dictate the worldview of those with no control of reality (objects).

Subjugation: The process of being conquered, enslaved, subdued, reduced, or defeated.

Suffrage: The right to vote.

Suppression: The process of being put down or held back by authority or force.

Truth vs. truth: Refers to the traditional/phallocentric/modernist idea of one reality (Truth) versus the nontraditional/feminist/postmodernist idea of multiple realities (truth).

Victimization: The process of being made a victim; to be repeatedly cheated, fooled, or injured.

Womyn: A term used by radical feminists to take the term "man" out of "woman," with the goal of raising awareness of language bias and the ways in which language shapes perceptions and ideas of gender and gender roles.

GOALS, ACTIVISM, AND MAJOR PROJECTS OF WOMEN'S STUDIES

Below are some of the major categories of **goals and activism** within the feminist community. Many of these categories include contradictory and diverse views of feminism and its aims.

Sexuality: Promote free sexual expression; change existing sexual paradigms; elevate status of clitoris; promote non-penetrative sex; include sex workers in feminist discourse about sexuality; protect sex workers' health and integrity; encourage more sexual pleasure for women; increase acceptance of non-heterosexual identities.

Rape: Raise awareness of sexual violence; fight for more legal protection of rape victims; change language surrounding rape; keep streets safe for women; change rape law; prosecute marital rape; demonstrate and march to show solidarity among women.

Body image: Change beauty standards; challenge thinness as single norm; accept all body types and sizes; fight rising epidemic of eating disorders; help women have better body self-esteem; encourage active lifestyles and healthy bodies; support athletic programs for women; discourage useless and sometimes harmful beauty practices; encourage natural bodies.

Pornography: Challenge laws about pornography; encourage healthy pornographic images; support women-made pornography; label pornography as a violation of women's civil rights; support censorship legislation; restrict distribution of pornography; encourage more dominatrix/woman-empowered pornography.

Marriage/weddings: Challenge existing wedding customs; look at subtext of marriage vows (domestic labor and sex in exchange for economic support); subvert the home as women's territory; subvert work as men's territory; change wedding customs that imply exchanging women between two men (e.g., father walking daughter down aisle, bride's parents paying for wedding).

Motherhood/childcare: Fight for equal childcare responsibilities; split domestic tasks evenly; fight for better maternity leave and illness policies; promote paternity leave; remove taboo from motherhood; think beyond the "Mommy Track."

Sex roles: Fight sex-role socialization at an early age; do not allow/force children to fall neatly into gender categories; challenge toy companies to make gender-neutral items; fight sexist advertising; boycott industries that indoctrinate girls into body hatred; challenge parenting manuals.

Domestic violence: Provide shelter for abused women; encourage community support for victims; raise awareness about prevalence of spousal abuse and rape; help women become economically independent; believe women when they report abuse; help women maintain a fair standard of living.

Bodies: Give women full control over their bodies; view women's bodies as active agents rather than passive receptacles; teach women to make peace with their bodies; educate young women about their changing bodies; protest beauty pageants; reject restrictive clothing; rethink negative cultural views of menstruation; challenge harmful body practices such as breast augmentation; challenge, in a self-reflexive way, harmful body practices outside the U.S. such as female genital mutilation and foot binding; educate about breast cancer; help women make decisions about their bodies in an educated manner; encourage body acceptance and body love.

Birth control: Educate women about birth control options; spread correct information about the relationship between high birth rates and low sex education; challenge pharmaceutical companies to develop safer and more effective birth control products; make all options available to all women.

Abortion: Give women the right to choose an abortion; educate women about proper birth control techniques; escort women who want an abortion into the clinic; protect doctors who perform abortions; encourage a climate of choice, allowing some women to be against abortion for themselves; challenge misinformation; protest anti-abortion legislation; fight for governmental funding for abortion agencies; protect reproductive freedom.

Economy/work: Value work traditionally done by women, including domestic labor and childcare; erase distinctions and value differences between kinds of work; allow women to work in all professions, including the military and all religious leadership positions; encourage women to work outside the home and men to work inside the home; challenge the fact that a woman makes 74 cents to a man's $1.00.

Women of color: Challenge racist tendencies of feminist movements; support and defend affirmative action; recognize key contributions by women of color; recognize that feminism emerged from abolition work; encourage scholarship by women outside of the United States and Britain.

Glass ceiling: Fight against the competitive labor market that prohibits women from climbing the economic ladder; challenge capitalism and corporate culture; make equal opportunity a reality; end the "invisible barrier" between men and women in the workplace; challenge sexual harassment.

Fight backlash: Challenge anti-feminist views; educate about the feminist movement; appropriate and alter negative language about women and feminism; challenge mainstream media representations of women; fight against women's oppression both domestically and globally; accept all forms of feminism as legitimate; encourage multiple interpretations of feminism; remember where feminism has been and where it is going.

INTELLECTUAL "STARS" OF WOMEN'S STUDIES

These categories, and the women represented in them, indicate the major shifts in feminist theory, scholarship, and intellectual community within the feminist movement over time.

Abolitionists
Sarah Mapps Douglass
Harriet Purvis
Lucretia Mott
Sarah & Margaretta Forten
Harriet Tubman

⇨

First-Wave Feminists
Susan B. Anthony
Elizabeth Cady Stanton
Lucy Stone
Alice Paul

⇨

Second-Wave Feminists
Betty Friedan
Gloria Steinem
Kate Millet
Germaine Greer
Redstockings

⇨

French Feminists
Julia Kristeva
Luce Irigaray
Hélène Cixous
Simone de Beauvoir
Monique Wittig

⇨

Radical Feminists
Valerie Solanas
Boston's Cell 16
Catherine MacKinnon
Andrea Dworkin
The Guerrilla Girls
Mary Daly

⇨

Third-Wave Feminists
Gayle Rubin
Robin Morgan
Judith Butler
Donna Haraway
Avital Ronell

⇨

Black Feminists
Patricia Hill Collins
bell hooks
Patricia Williams
Angela Davis
Audre Lorde

⇨

Standpoint Feminists
Nancy Hartstock
Sandra Harding
Julia Wood
Dorothy Smith
Hilary Rose

⇨

Third-World Feminists
Gayatri Spivak
Trinh T. Minh-Ha
Gloria Anzaldua
Seyla Benhabib
Chandra Talpade Mohanty
Chela Sandoval

SPARKCHARTS™

7 20593 02715 3

WOMEN'S STUDIES

INTRODUCTION TO WOMEN'S STUDIES

The wide-ranging, interdisciplinary field of **women's studies** has been propelled by **feminism**—a broad concept that encompasses many definitions and goals.

DEFINITIONS OF FEMINISM

1. **Challenging** the power structure between men and women; seeing men and women as groups rather than individuals.
2. **Rebelling** against and rejecting power structures, institutions, laws, or social conventions that maintain women as subordinate, powerless, or second-class citizens.
3. **Arguing** against the division of labor that values men in the public sphere (work, sports, government, law, war) and devalues women in the private sphere (home, child care, reproductive labor, housework, maintaining family).
4. **Working** as a collective to fight for women's rights in all facets of modern life, including the workplace, sexuality, reproductive rights, fair representation, and acceptance of alternative families.
5. **Demanding** full rights for all women and men.

GOALS OF FEMINISM

1. **Provide multiple narratives** of women's history, beyond the typical white, male story.
2. **View "sex" and "gender" as fluid** instead of fixed, as social rather than biological.
3. **Fight for equality and raise awareness** of the challenges women face in their lives.
4. **Make both men and women aware** of gender inequality and the way it harms society.
5. **Critique the institutions** (i.e., schools, government, workplace) that support patriarchy.
6. **Dismantle** discriminatory policies and laws.
7. **Encourage "choice"** in multiple arenas (i.e., marriage, reproduction, work).
8. **Include sexuality** at the forefront of women's issues.
9. **Accept multiple forms of feminism** (i.e., not everyone has the same definition)
10. **Continually revise feminism** and its aims.

MAJOR EVENTS IN WOMEN'S HISTORY

ANCIENT TIMES: 900 BCE–1300s CE

Up to 900 BCE, human cultures are primarily nomadic. Some **division of labor** exists, but tasks are assigned equal social and cultural value. From 900–600 BCE, the **Middle Assyrian Code** of law limits women, enforcing fidelity, veiling, and arranged marriages. As **farming cultures** emerge over the period from 600 BCE–1300 CE, women become objects of trade, and their freedoms are restricted further.

THE FEUDAL SYSTEM: 1300s–1700s

Kings, nobles, and clerics rule over artisans, merchants, and peasants, while individuals support themselves through work done close to the home, primarily on farms. **Women's labor** differs from men's, but men and women work together. No designed value is placed on "women's work" vs. "men's work."

INDUSTRIALIZATION: 1700s

The rise of manufacturing and larger cities separate work from home. The idea of a **male "breadwinner"** and the economically-dependent **"housewife"** emerge, and new **social classes** form: laborers without land and urban middle-class landowners. Under English common law (coverture), women belong legally to their husbands during marriage and cannot own property.
- Voltaire, Locke, Jefferson, Montesquieu, and others make the **quest for freedom** their central intellectual focus. As these male scholars challenge tyranny and "divine rights," women begin to question the tyranny of men over women.
- The **French Revolution** challenges social inequalities and opens doors for women's fight for equality. In October 1789, 6,000 working-class women march on government offices in Paris demanding cheaper bread.
- **Mary Wollstonecraft's** *A Vindication of the Rights of Woman* (1792) argues against domestic tyranny, saying that women's financial dependence on men is "legal prostitution" and that differences between the sexes should be abolished.

EARLY FEMINISM: 1800s

As **slavery** in America becomes widespread in the early 1800s, many scholars and activists challenge its existence, and the **Underground Railroad** is set up to help slaves come to freedom. Women in this period are largely confined to the home and are expected to marry in order to secure status and privilege. In the 1870s and 1880s, **social purity feminism** emerges, arguing against alcohol, violence, and sexual excess as masculine evils that threaten women and families. **Victorian ideals of** womanhood reign, emphasizing chastity, upkeep of the home, and raising of children.

1833	Lucretia Mott and others form the **Female Antislavery Society**
1840	Elizabeth Cady Stanton and Lucretia Mott serve as U.S. delegates to the World Antislavery Convention
1848	Stanton and Mott call the first **Seneca Falls Convention** for women's rights; draft the *Seneca Falls Declaration of Sentiments*, which calls for women's right to vote and states that all men and women are created equal
	Married Women's Property Acts (New York State) give women more property rights
1850–1860	14 states pass property-law reforms, giving women some rights to own property and land (rights that earlier were forfeited upon marriage)
1851	**Susan B. Anthony** begins to campaign with Stanton for women's rights, education, right to divorce, women's property rights, careers for women, and right to vote
1852	First women's rights convention to list suffrage as its goal is convened
1865	**13th Amendment** emancipates slaves in the U.S.
1868	**14th Amendment** guarantees that all Americans have equal protection under the law
1869	Wyoming becomes first U.S. territory to pass a law permitting women to vote

1870	**15th Amendment** gives black men the right to vote, further inspiring the women's suffrage movement
	Wyoming allows women to serve on juries
1873	Supreme Court rules that married women can be excluded from practicing law
1874	Supreme Court upholds ruling that women should be denied the right to vote
1880s	Darwin's theory of **evolution** offers alternative explanation for male-female inequalities, shifting from the "Adam's rib" explanation to a more scientifically based explanation of female inferiority
1884	**Friedrich Engels's** *The Origins of the Family, Private Property, and the State* challenges ethnographic and historical evidence of women's inferiority. Engels argues that women and men were equal in prehistoric times and that gender inequality originated with the advent of private property.
1890	National American Woman Suffrage Association founded to work toward securing voting rights
1890s	**Psychoanalysis** emerges as major theoretical and therapeutic movement
1893	Colorado grants women the right to vote
1896	National Association of Colored Women founded

FIRST-WAVE FEMINISM: 1900s–1920s

By 1900, **suffragettes** are at the forefront of the women's rights movement, campaigning heavily for voting rights. By the 1920s, most girls in Europe and North America receive primary school education, while upper and upper-middle-class women go to universities. Also in the 1920s, feminism takes the form of **alternative style trends** such as flapper dresses and short haircuts, and "masculine" behaviors like smoking and drinking alcohol.

1908	Supreme Court upholds Oregon's 10-hour workday for women
1911	Term "feminism" first used
1916	Jeannette Rankin (R-MT) becomes the first woman elected to Congress
	Margaret Sanger opens the first **birth control clinic**
1918	Sanger wins court case allowing doctors to counsel women on birth control options
1920	League of Women Voters formed
	19th Amendment grants women the right to vote
	Women's bureau set up in the Department of Labor
1921	Sheppard-Towner Maternity and Infancy Protection Act
1922	**Cable Act** guarantees a woman's nationality independent of her husband's
1923	**Equal Rights Amendment** first introduced in Congress
1924	Congress grants Native Americans citizenship
1929	**Stock market crashes**, sending financial world into chaos and beginning the Great Depression

DEPRESSION AND WAR: 1930s–1950s

In the 1930s, the **Great Depression** creates economic hardship, with unemployment, poverty, and unrest. Women who are employed face resentment for "stealing" men's work. When the U.S. becomes involved in **World War II** in 1941, seven million women go to work for the first time while men go to war. These jobs range from riveters (inspiring the image of "Rosie the Riveter") to baseball players. After the war, 80 percent of women want to keep their new jobs, but men force women out of the workplace and back into the home. Media images of the 1950s aggressively encourage women to stay at home and be happy, subservient housewives. The 1950s also see the advent of **mother-blaming**, helped along by new developments in **psychoanalysis**. New theories blame "bad" mothers for alcoholism, crime, delinquency, rape, and a host of men's problems (sexual inadequacies, fears, worries, or homosexual inclinations).

1932	**Federal Economy Act** forbids more than one member of the same family from working for the government, causing many women to lose their jobs (enforced until 1937)
1935	**Social Security Act** gives federal benefits to widows and dependent children
1938	**Fair Labor Standards Act** upholds minimum wage regardless of sex
1942	Women's branches established in the military
1943	First government-funded daycare centers and nurseries founded
1947	Supreme Court rules that women may serve on juries
1950	Senate subcommittee rules that homosexuals should not be recruited to the U.S. government
1953	**Simone de Beauvoir** becomes the feminist voice of the 1950s as she retraces the history of women in *The Second Sex* (first published in France in 1949)
	Alfred Kinsey publishes *Sexual Behavior in the Human Female*
1954	*Brown vs. Board of Education* bans school segregation
1955	**Rosa Parks's** refusal to vacate a "whites only" bus seat in Montgomery, AL, prompts black and white women to join together to fight segregation

SECOND-WAVE FEMINISM: 1960s

In the early 1960s, many middle- and upper-class white women begin to question their **domestic roles**—a phenomenon that becomes known as "the problem that has no name." In the late 1960s, a **culture of revolution** emerges, with protests against the Vietnam War, formation of the lesbian separatist communities, student protests in Europe, guerrilla movements in Latin America, liberation struggles in Africa, a cultural revolution in China, and a tide of socialism and Marxism. This culture fuels the strength of the women's movement going into the 1970s.

1960	Southern blacks found Student Nonviolent Coordinating Committee to protest civil rights abuses
	Birth control pills approved for sale in the U.S.
1961	John F. Kennedy establishes President's Commission on the Status of Women, chaired by Eleanor Roosevelt
1963	**Betty Friedan** writes bestseller *The Feminine Mystique*, which questions the "cult of domesticity" and asks women to reconsider their inferior social roles
	JFK appoints a permanent Citizens' Advisory Council on the Status of Women
	Equal Pay Act provides equitable pay for women
1964	**Civil Rights Act** and **Title VII** prohibit employment discrimination based on race, color, religion, national origin, or sex; **Equal Employment Opportunity Commission** is created to enforce Title VII
1965	Labor laws altered to allow more equal work conditions and more jobs for women
	Supreme Court rules that married couples can use **birth control**
	Helen Gurley Brown transforms *Cosmopolitan* into a women's magazine
1966	**National Organization of Women (NOW)** founded
	Lyndon B. Johnson's administration approves first federal family planning funding
1967	Conference on New Politics in Chicago drops feminist resolution from its agenda, sparking criticism
	Chicago Women's Liberation Group formed; likely the first to use the term "liberation" with regard to women
	New York Radical Women founded; first radical feminist group
	Affirmative action first extended to women
	American Civil Liberties Union challenges sodomy laws
	California legalizes **abortion**

MAJOR EVENTS IN WOMEN'S HISTORY (continued)

1968	Protests against **Miss America** pageant draw media coverage and reports of "bra-burning women's libbers"
	NOW bill of rights published
	Women's Equity Action League established
	First **feminist publications** appear in the U.S. (approximately 500 appear between 1968–1973)
	Shirley Chisholm (D-NY) becomes first African-American woman elected to Congress
	National Abortion Rights Action League formed
1969	Conference on Women held at Cornell University
	First large-scale **women's studies** course offered (at Cornell University)
	Woodstock Music and Art Fair in Sullivan County, NY
	Rita Mae Brown resigns from NOW in protest of group's stance on lesbianism
	Women's health book *Our Bodies, Ourselves* first published by the Boston Women's Health Book Collective

HEIGHT OF THE MOVEMENT: 1970s

In the 1970s, women convene **consciousness-raising groups** to educate about gender oppression, create community, and share common experiences. The first **women's studies departments** are developed at universities, and the United Nations designates the 1970s the "Women's Decade." However, some **black women** challenge the women's movement as failing to acknowledge non-white concerns, and many become disillusioned. **Lesbian feminists** challenge the women's movement to reconsider their attitudes toward the nuclear family, calling upon women to become "political lesbians" and stop "sleeping with the enemy."

1970	Equal Rights Amendment reintroduced to Congress
	Kate Millett publishes *Sexual Politics*
	Sit-ins at *Newsweek* and *Ladies Home Journal* staged to protest discrimination against women workers
	Chicana feminists found Comisión Feminil Mexicana
	Betty Friedan resigns from NOW, calls for women's strike to mark 50th anniversary of 19th Amendment
	California adopts a "no-fault" divorce law
	Radical feminist groups "Redstockings" and "Radicalesbians" founded
	Germaine Greer publishes *The Female Eunuch*
	Robin Morgan publishes *Sisterhood is Powerful*
	Pat Mainardi proposes "wages for housework"
1971	New York Radical Women organize first public "speak-outs" on rape
	Ms. magazine debuts as an insert in *New York* magazine
1972	**Title IX** prohibits sex discrimination in public education
	Supreme Court rules that right to privacy includes use of birth control by single people (couples won use in 1965)
	Equal Rights Amendment (ERA) passes in the Senate
	Conservative activist **Phyllis Schlafly** forms Stop ERA

1973	**Roe vs. Wade** grants women abortion rights
	Supreme Court bans sex categorizing in employment ads
	American Psychiatric Association officially removes homosexuality from the category of mental illness
	30 states ratify the ERA
1974	**Equal Credit Opportunity Act** forbids racial or sexual discrimination in the credit industry
	Women's Educational Equity Act establishes non-sexist and nondiscriminatory vocational programs
	Maternity laws revised to prohibit discrimination based on pregnancy
	Ella Grasso elected first female governor (D-CT)
1975	Susan Brownmiller publishes *Against Our Will: Men, Women, and Rape*
	First issue of *Signs* published
	Supreme Court rules that states must allow women jurors
1976	Court equalizes drinking age for men and women
	U.S. military academies open admissions to women
	Supreme Court rules that fathers cannot veto daughters' abortion decisions
1977	First National Women's Conference held in Houston
	National Women's Studies Association founded
1978	Congress passes **Pregnancy Discrimination Act** to prohibit job discrimination against pregnant women
	Massive march on Washington, D.C., in support of ERA
	First "Take Back the Night" march for rape awareness
1979	TV evangelist Jerry Falwell founds the Moral Majority
	5,000 feminists march against pornography in New York

BACKLASH ERA: 1980s

The 1980s and the Reagan years saw a **backlash** against feminism and the **defeat of the Equal Rights Amendment**.

1980	Republican party platform drops support of ERA and denounces abortion
	Abortion drug **RU-486** developed in France
1981	Supreme Court rules that women can be excluded from the **military draft**
	Supreme Court overturns law that husband is "head and master" of women's property
	Sandra Day O'Connor becomes first woman appointed to the Supreme Court
1982	Carol Gilligan publishes *In a Different Voice*
	ERA fails and is not ratified
1983	**Sally Ride** becomes the first American woman in space
	Supreme Court rules that minors need **parental consent** before seeking abortions
1984	Supreme Court forbids sex discrimination in social and other organizations (such as Elks and Jaycees)
	Geraldine Ferraro becomes first female VP candidate

1986	Meese Commission finds pornography "harmful" and a "social menace"
	Supreme Court rules that a hostile work environment qualifies as sex discrimination
1987	Supreme Court rules that legal decisions can account for sex and race
1988	**Civil Rights Restoration Act** restores full coverage of Title IX
1989	Supreme Court rules that states can deny public funding for abortions and abortion clinics

THIRD-WAVE FEMINISM: 1990s

In the 1990s, fierce **abortion debates** create deep partisan divisions about funding, counseling, late-term abortion, and the state's "compelling" interest in potential human life.

1991	Clarence Thomas accused of sexual harassment
1992	Colorado, Oregon pass **anti-gay laws** (overturned in 1996)
1993	**Family and Medical Leave Act** gives men and women protected unpaid leave to deal with family emergencies
	Shannon Faulkner admitted to the Citadel and later kicked out after her gender is discovered
	Supreme Court rules that no serious psychological or physical injury is needed to prove sexual harassment
1994	Supreme Court rules that obstruction of an abortion clinic is a crime
	Violence Against Women Act provides services for victims of rape and domestic violence, and establishes a 24-hour hotline service
1995	Wal-Mart removes a shirt that says "Someday a woman will be President" from its shelves on the grounds that it is "anti-family"
1996	Supreme Court rules that the Citadel and Virginia Military Institute must open admissions to women
	Eve Ensler's *Vagina Monologues* first performed
1997	Supreme Court rules that in order for schools to receive Title IX funding, equal numbers of men and women must participate in sports
1998	Class-action lawsuit against Mitsubishi settles for $34 million after multiple claims of sexual harassment

2000s: 9/11 AND BEYOND

2000	CBS agrees to pay $8 million to settle a sex discrimination lawsuit on behalf of 200 women
2003	**Iraq War** sees increase in female military involvement
	Congress passes **partial-birth abortion ban**
	Supreme Court overturns **sodomy laws**, legalizing consenting sexual behavior between adults
2004	Massachusetts legalizes **gay marriage**
	March for Women's Lives in Washington, D.C., protests Bush policies on abortion and women's healthcare

PROMINENT WOMEN IN HISTORY

Hatshepsut	1400s BCE	Considered most successful ruler of Egypt
Nefertiti	1300s BCE	Egyptian queen; espoused monotheistic religion
Helen of Troy	unknown	Greek; renowned for beauty, involvement in Trojan War
Semiramis	800s BCE	Assyrian queen, architect; rebuilt Babylon and Nineveh
Sappho	610–640 BCE	Greek lyric poet from island of Lesbos
Aspasia	400s BCE	Anatolian scholar, orator, high-class courtesan, lecturer
Cleopatra	69–30 BCE	Egyptian queen; protected against Romans
Boadicea	c. 25–62 CE	British warrior queen; defied Roman conquerors
Phung Thi Chinh	c. 40 CE	Led Vietnamese army of resistance against Chinese
Trung sisters	died 43	Defenders and rulers of Vietnam; committed suicide
Pan Chao	c. 45–115	Foremost female scholar in China; devoted to literature
Mary the Jewess	c. 50	Egyptian alchemist and inventor
Aelia Galla Placidia	c. 388–450	Roman empress; daughter of Theodosius I
Hypatia	c. 365–415	Egyptian philosopher and mathematician
Theodora	c. 497–548	Byzantine performer; married Roman Emperor Justinian I
Wu Chao	625–705	Chinese concubine-turned-empress; spread Buddhism
Bathilde	c. 630–680	English slave-turned-queen; outlawed slavery
Murasaki Shikibu	c. 978–1030	Japanese; wrote *Tale of Genji* (first full-length novel)
Anna Comnena	c. 1083–1148	Byzantine historian; wrote the *Alexiad*; criticized Crusades
Héloïse	1098–1164	French; tragic lover-turned-nun; wife of Pierre Abélard
Hildegard of Bingen	1098–1179	German theologian, writer, Church advisor
Eleanor of Aquitaine	1122–1204	Wife of Louis VII; aided wounded soldiers
Tamara of Georgia	died 1212	Georgian builder and queen during Golden Age
Blanche of Castile	1188–1252	English wife of Louis VIII; stopped Henry III's invasion
Christine de Pisan	1364–1430	French-Italian poet, historian, social critic
Margery Kempe	1373–1438	English religious enthusiast; first known autobiography
Jadwiga	1373–1399	Polish queen; united Poland and Lithuania
Joan of Arc	1412–1431	French religious warrior; executed at age 19
Isabella I	1451–1504	Queen of Spain and Aragon; allied with New World

Lucrezia Borgia	1480–1519	Italian noblewoman; daughter of Pope Alexander VI
La Malinche	c. 1500–1527	Mexican; helped Cortés conquer Mexico
Ann Boleyn	1507–1536	Wife of Henry VIII; beheaded for inability to produce son
"Bloody" Mary Tudor	1516–1558	English; daughter of Henry VIII; anti-Protestant Catholic
Catherine de Médicis	1519–1589	Italian-French; wed Henry II; tried to settle religious wars
Elizabeth I	1533–1603	British Queen; inspired English Renaissance
Mary, Queen of Scots	1542–1587	Scottish; famed Queen and devout Catholic; beheaded
Artemisia Gentileschi	1593–c. 1652	Italian painter; follower of Caravaggio's Baroque style
Anne Bradstreet	1612–1672	English-American Puritan poet
Christina of Sweden	1626–1689	Swedish queen and arts patron; abdicated throne
Aphra Behn	1640–1689	English dramatist, poet; first English woman paid author
Sor Juana Inés de la Cruz	1651–1695	Mexican scholar, poet, nun; first Latin American poet
Emilie du Châtelet	1706–1749	French mathematician and physicist; mistress of Voltaire
Madame du Pompadour	1721–1764	Mistress of Louis XV; built École Militaire in Paris
Catherine the Great	1729–1796	German-born empress of Russia for 34 years; reformer
Olympia de Gouges	1748–1793	French; social reformer; author of anti-slave trade plays
Marie-Antoinette	1755–1793	Extravagant French queen; overthrown during Revolution
Mary Wollstonecraft	1759–1797	English activist, writer (*A Vindication of the Rights of Woman*)
Deborah Sampson	1760–1827	American Revolutionary soldier, lecturer
Théroigne de Méricourt	1766–1817	Critic of the French Revolution
Emma Willard	1787–1870	American educator; fought for girls' schools and colleges
Grimké sisters	1800s	American abolitionists, daughters of plantation owner
Lucretia Mott	1793–1880	American abolitionist, Quaker; women's rights advocate
Sojourner Truth	c. 1797–1883	American abolitionist; wrote *Ain't I a Woman?* speech (1851)
Dorothea Dix	1802–1887	American social reformer on behalf of mentally ill
Harriet Beecher Stowe	1811–1896	American philanthropist; wrote *Uncle Tom's Cabin*
Elizabeth Cady Stanton	1815–1902	American suffragette, organizer of Seneca Falls Convention
Lucy Stone	1818–1893	American activist, pioneer of suffrage movement
Maria Mitchell	1818–1889	American; first professional woman astronomer

CONTINUED ON OTHER SIDE